words.love

A Compilation of Poetry by
Ingrid Turner

Ingrid Turner
words.love
© 2019, Ingrid Turner
Self-published
ingrid@ingridturner.com
ISBN-13: 978-1-7332962-0-5

All rights reserved.
No part of this publication may be reproduced, stored in a retrieval system, stored in a database and / or published in any form or by any means, electronic, mechanical, photocopying, recording or otherwise, without the prior written permission of the publisher.

For my mother, Vilina: the
first person I send every new
poem to: my most ardent
supporter in the arts.

I love you, mom.

A Word of Deepest Thanks

Generally, one entity cannot create life, and that's certainly true of this book.

A whole team came together for this; some I asked, and some swooped in and left me delighted with their comments and guidance.

First, my mother, who deserves years of gushing gratitude for her support, for which she'll never get her due. She also assisted with some of the most frustrating technical pieces of this manuscript, plus editing.

My partner, Dwayne, the truly artistic one of our couple-dom, who helped me iron out a solid direction for cover design. Then came the online tribe, who tightened up the whole thing with their loving and experienced feedback: Marita, Jaya, Barbara, Charlotte, Amber, Joanne, Shari, Rebecca, and more whom I'm not able to name here.

And the Bhava Spiritual Mission Leadership Ministry…you all inspire me every day to live in faith, act on inspiration, and be fearless in the pursuit of divine joy. You are my biggest cheerleaders in all I do. I love you, I appreciate you, more than words can possibly express: Lou, Joseph, Harmony, Charlotte, Celeste, Torsten, Ian, Mary, Yvonne, Rebecca, Lydia, Marita, and Vicki.

There are so many people, I have so much support, and I can't possibly get it all here on paper. I am so grateful - beyond grateful - for the beautiful humans who grace my life and work.

Table of Contents

Introduction 1

A Fight 5

A Note from God 7

A Pause 8

An Offer or Request 10

Bad Lover 12

Best Admired From a Distance 15

Brave 17

Crema 19

Crimi 20

Dancing in the Kitchen 21

Delusion 22

Dementia 23

Divine Sin 25

Dreamers Are Never Satisfied 26

Forever Forever 27

For Us 28

God, Are You Hiring? 30

How I Grew My Wings 32

How Can It Be? 33

In Contradiction I am Home 34

I Am Love 35

I Know Why Hemingway Wrote 36

I Will Break You 37

I'll Meet You in Poetry 41

It's Better from a Distance 42

It's Not That 46

Joey 48

Johanna 49

Just Between You and Me 51

Laughing in the Sky 52

Love Robs Me of Words 53

Me Loving Me 55

WORDS.LOVE

Monster Attacks a City 56

My Beautiful Things 57

One-Way Ticket 58

Our Fight 59

Piano 60

Prayer 62

Quit 63

Rebel 64

Rings 66

Savior 68

Siren Song 69

Stasis No More 70

Suzanne 71

Swallows Her Tears 73

Sweet Surrender 76

That Scent 78

The Flowers Are Pink 79

The Man and the Genie 81

Time in Love 84

Today I Walk with the Lord 86

Tribute to a Troubled Father 87

Two Become One 88

Untitled 89

When the Dawn Breaks 90

Wretched 91

You Can't Bottle Magic 92

Introduction

Where do I start but with my forever love of poetry?

I was the elementary school kid hauling a backpack full of notebooks and pens everywhere I went, scribbling in very poor scrawl, huddled in the back of the family's roaring Landcruiser. I was the teenager who squealed with delight when I unwrapped 'The Complete Works of William Blake' on Christmas morning.

For as long as I can remember, I have devoured lyricism through every possible medium - poetry encyclopedias have lined my bookshelf since I was a teenager. The Internet opened me up to modern, faster, broader, more diverse authors. Social media enabled to me to drink in the poetry of my peers, and provided a platform for me to share my own. Music is a where I began to understand the rhythm of poetry.

Words are an intuitive part of me: there is nothing technical about my poetry. It follows a rhythm of which perhaps only I am aware. I have a basic American education, but I am a keen listener, watcher, and learner of life. My path is not mainstream, and neither is my poetry.

I wrote my first poem when I was seven years old. An image crashed like a flash flood into my brain and I could do nothing until I put the words on paper. And it's always been like that: many of my poems are unrelated to my own life, or are from a completely different point of view - perhaps that of a man or a lifestyle with which I have never identified. But this is how the muse shows up for me: whispering one line, pouring vivid imagery into my mind, and I am at the mercy of the poem. I feel I can hardly claim ownership of the words you're about to read on these pages.

Poetry makes me vulnerable. Just about all artists experience this with their medium. There is a raw, under-developed piece of us that feels exposed in our work, and few of us have the courage to continue to create without the love, guidance, and support of others.

For me, that guidance came most strongly from my parents. Had my parents not been keenly interested and complimentary of my 7-year-old self's budding exploration of poetry, I would have stopped right there. But the interested questions, the compliments, and validation from the two most important people in my world kept me going with this work.

I have many memories of helpful, encouraging conversations with my father, Josef, in regards to my writing before he died. He told me about the Thesaurus (yaaaas!) and shared about his favorite authors and stories.

But it has been my mother, Vilina, throughout the decades who has been the bedrock of my creative courage. She is the first person I send every new poem to, full insecurity raging in her direction:

'Is it good? Do you like it?'

Her encouragement, validation, and patience with my artistic neediness is what brought you and I here today. I am quite sure that without her, I would not have found it in me to share my raw, exposed core with the world.

I am so grateful to be here, courageous, yes, and afraid, and, for the first time, sharing my true love: poetry. This book seems to be a lifetime in the making, and includes only a fraction of my full body of work - much of which I have lost.

INGRID TURNER

Thank you for coming along on this
journey with me.

A Fight

Half way across the street
(thinking in pictures)

Found himself the target
of a nasty metal heap.

The clunker slammed to a halt
(a breath in front of him),

Rusty doors screamed,
revealing some chesty preening.

Mad Men! Mad Men!
(do they swagger or do they limp?)

Surrounded this picture guy
in the middle of the street.

Glowering and growling
(huffling and puffling)

Narrowed eyes and flexing jaws:

Picture man fights today.

From the front, from left
(that guy's behind you!)

A palm to the jaw handles you
a kick to the groin buckles you.

Elbow behind his head
(noses make a mighty crunch)

Swing that thug right round
Did he smash the fucking window

Or what!?

Back in the middle of the street
(never broke eye contact)

Picture man is grinning
addled boys scramble off

(unharmed).

So, picture man:
he crosses the street today.

A Note from God

I've always said yes.

You've never had to beg or plead

It's always been yes.

You never needed faith.

You never needed anything at all.

How could I deny such creation?

A Pause

I have to apologize to you:

For when you kindly included me
over the Holiday ruckus;

'What have you been up to?'

I'm sorry my voice caught,
while I held your anticipative gaze.

I was trying to reconcile this year
in the few lines you expect from me.

Can I tell you about communing with
my *soul*?
Can I share about my God-Heart?

Or about my *un*-schooling
in energy and vibration?

Will you stay with me when I tell you,
I've been working on letting *time*

        …sweep me away with her?

Let me tell you about the visions!

I'll need miles of canvas to paint
those dreams.

Can I explain to you what it feels like
when the dead send their love?

WORDS.LOVE

Truth be told, friend,
I've spent so little time on Earth
this year.

I don't have an answer,
in the box I think you want from me.

So, I apologize,
for this awkward lapse in time

While I'm searching for an answer
and wondering if

        …you really want to talk
   about it?

But maybe I can take you dimension
hopping
one of these days.

And then

        …we'll really talk about
   it.

An Offer or Request

You're crazy up there
spinning notes and penning poesy

In all your sultry madness
painting with your messy innards.

It's required of all the greats
who dictate from Celeste.

I got your love note
doubled me over in a dream.

And I'm happily drowning
in your oceanic depths.

We've mingled spirits for a spell
Deep. Palpable. Carnal.

'Dear God, give me more'
I've moaned and moaned.

I love you.

I do. I do.

But there's an impasse ahead
questions to face.

I've got this offer for you
or a request, if you prefer:

WORDS.LOVE

Will you run naked with the wolves
by my side through snow and sleet?

I'm bounding toward the edge
for a swan dive off the bluff.

Will you hold my hand
and make it a lovers' leap?

My sword is drawn
I've become the beast.

Will you charge the gates
and match my scream?

Dear love, my soul
will you, will you?

I will be running

and leaping

and baring my teeth

I'll be banging on gates
and wrestling the deep.

I'll do it on my own if I must
shaking under destiny's stars.

But I would accept a little refuge
in your warm, kindred heart.

Bad Lover

You were sinewed with me
weren't you?

All tangled up in my mess

Telling me how relieved I felt
by your vinegar kiss.

Mmmm, and I believed you for so long.

Until you made me crazy.

Or was I already crazy?

And you just rode along?

Egged me on?

You know, people don't like me
because of you.

I remember
that rush to get home.

To kick off my heels,
and meet you in the kitchen.

Wrap my hands around your neck.

You purred when I got home
and we sat for hours.

Barefoot. Hand in hand.

WORDS.LOVE

Until you made me sad.
Or mad.

Or was I already those things
masked by our heady conversation?

I snuck home sometimes at lunch,
just to see you.

To touch your lips and slip away.

But you really started in, didn't
you?

All that touching

Understanding

Waiting for me, enticing me.

I believed in you!

But I think they call that gas
lighting.

Controlling. Abusive, even.

Intoxicating? Without a doubt.

Addiction? I met the criteria.

Oh, you horrible trickster.
I would have sworn you cared.

And now I talk about you
like a disease.

I replaced you with a whole group of people
to fill that hole.

And we talk about you
all the time.

I still long for you, sometimes.
I see you out there, sometimes.

On a restaurant patio table.
or peeking into a bar.

You're making everyone laugh
like you made me laugh, before.

Anyone can be your friend, I guess.

But never your lover.

WORDS.LOVE

Best Admired From a Distance

That one is best admired from a
distance.

Yes, she's got those
rumbling curves and flashy eyes.

Her smile will make you wilt
and stand taller, still.

I suppose if you must approach
keep her well contained.

But you watch her close, now!

Go on - enjoy her, for a while.
She'll stay put for a time.

But eventually, you'll see
she's scraping her chains against
rock.

Gnashing and writhing: she's bleeding
for freedom.

You can try and keep her longer.
But I'm telling you, boy

In the end

She'll rip you apart.

INGRID TURNER

Yes, boy,
that one is best admired from a
distance.

Brave

Be well. Farewell. Have a good one.
    Aloha. Adios.

I never want to see your fucking face
again.

I'm saying all of these things
and, in parting, this:

    Be brave.

Be. Fucking. Brave.
Go after those demons with everything
you've got.

Don't let anything else slip and
slide between your fingers
    because you can't look
  that devil in the eye.

Be brave.
Storm the gate that seals your doom.

Combat mano-a-mano
    that fiend
  that's got you by the tail.

Be stupid brave.
Hold on in the rain so the lightning
strikes you.

Dive head first into that lake of
fire

                    damn the jagged rocks
            that'll crack your head open.

Be recklessly heroic
Don't walk – *run* into the black.

Stand unsteady at the top of the
needle
            see the world, *brave one*,
        and risk the fall.

And when the demon drops you
            and doom is released

And when the fiend devours you
            and the lightning blasts
you

And when the lake drowns you
            and the black takes you

And you when you fall, my love
            drifting to your death

The skies will rumble
        with your triumphant
    laugh!

                    ...Be brave, my love.

Defeat yourself.

Crema

'I'm so ready for the real'
she sighs, selecting Crema overtones.

'I need it raw'
she weeps, rubbing lotion into her thighs.

Craving essence, she really is
while she clutches a blanket to her shoulders.

Her nudity ruined
by stretches and dimples.

'Love me for me!'
she takes a verbal stand

And eats food she hates
and moves in ways that hurt.

Sobbing
standing over the scale.

Crimb

She walked in
and pierced.

Two flames became one.

He watched her
and collided

Two stars became one.

Plates shifted, and drew
lighthouses to each other.

Two lights in the night became one.

Over the surf and through the rocks
across continents.

No ship can steer wrong
with two burning as one.

Hold the vision, hold the wheel!
Praise the storm that draws us in.

Two guides came together,
to teach us as one.

Dancing in the Kitchen

I guess it was just after midnight

We were a little wired from the heat
and skittering delight.

We're getting to know each other
slowly

Inch by inch
Minute by minute
Night by night.

I stood strangely in the kitchen
my arms were crossed
because I'm afraid of this.

You leaned in with easy confidence.
Rocking.

Immutably, you rocked me
Swayed me
Played me.

You danced in my kitchen,
As if it were your own.

Delusion

Strength enough
to break it open
release the truth. Light!

No matter how blinding
hold the fortitude
to sit with terror

Until it's release
wavy
in smoky serenity.

Dementia

Photos line that wall
on the left.

The black and white ones
start at the beginning.

You can see Grandma in most of those.

She's got the obvious red lips
even on black and white.

She was really pretty, wasn't she?

She had more than red lips
and a pencil skirt.

There's a shine to that woman.

A firecracker in her eye
spices in her mouth

All rubbed into her hips.

She gets one on you, kiddo.
You don't get one on her.

'*That's* Grandma?'
The youngest is asking.

It's hard to reconcile
yesterday's mirthful gleam

With today's soft stare.

INGRID TURNER

Yes, that's Grandma honey.

The little one looks like
maybe he doesn't quite believe you.

He knows some things, you know.

Like...

Grandma doesn't say much.
But she screams when you bathe her.

Grandma doesn't move much
but she broke the lamp when she threw it.

Grandma doesn't know daddy
she thinks he's Grandpa

(who died a long time ago).

Grandma has to wear a diaper
and he doesn't have to any more.

He knows that Grandma is sad
and it makes him sad, too.

Especially when you tell him
that pretty lady in the picture...

That's Grandma.

Divine Sin

A foundation of obstinance
holds firm

The flowering of the divine
in you.

Dreamers Are Never Satisfied

Dreamers are never satisfied.

As wide as cosmic wings expand
As high as Mount Olympus stands
As loud as Thor's hammer cracks
As fierce as Kali's stance defies

This is the distance dreamers travel

But where none arrive

(least of all the dreamer).

Forever Forever

When all we've got left
is words

Remember, you and me fly
through stars.

If the space between us fills
with years

We'll never have to release
our hearts.

You and me and stars and free
forever forever.

INGRID TURNER

For Us

For us
    our love is
dancing to a symphony
    on a great stage.

So many rehearsals
    grinding through hours
scraping by screeching notes
    and deaf tones.

For us
    our love bas been
a lifetime of trips
    and falls

Twisted ankles and jammed toes.

For us
    our love is
a performance masterpiece!
    a tour-de-force in grace

And lilting intimacy.

Step by step.
Beat by beat.

For us
    our love is
hardly paying attention.
    to the moves, to the sounds

WORDS.LOVE

Lightly touching the horns and
violins
fingertip to fingertip.

A crescendo!

Feet fly across the stage.

The conductor
furious.
Frenzied.

The audience can't follow us here.

For us
     our love has been
years of falls and tears
     hours of repetition in motion.

There's no catching us in our finest
fusion.

For us
     our love is
Body.
     Mind.
          Heart.

God, Are You Hiring?

Hello *Lord*!

I'm writing to inquire about a job.

God, are you hiring?

See, I've lost someone awful dear to me

He's supposed to be in heaven with you.

I miss him terribly and, well,
I thought if I made myself useful

Perhaps I could work for you
and spend my breaks with him?

I know I don't have the
qualifications, per se -

No angel wings yet,
and I am still firmly on the ground.

WORDS.LOVE

But God, I can assure you
I'm a real hard worker and I learn
quick.

I have the references to prove it!

So, God, if you're hiring
for anything at all

I'll start right at the bottom
and work my way up.

It's just awful important to me
and I do appreciate your
consideration

Even without all the experience and
degrees.

So, God, are you hiring?

And may I have an application,
please?

How I Grew My Wings

'Move closer to the edge.'
The voice says.

'I can't.'
My feet tremble.

'Move closer to the edge.'
The voice insists.

'I can't.'
My stomach whirls.

'Move closer to the edge.'
The voice demands.

'I can't.'
Now gravity pulls me.

I step.

I fall.

And that is how I grew my wings.

How Can It Be?

How can it be?

That time and experience
stand at such odds

And tell the same story
of 'I love you'?

How can it be?

That two sides of the Universe
glimpsed each other

And said *I do*.

How can it be?

That curling through life
has led me to you

And you to me?

And finally, you must tell me

How can it be?

That I love you this deeply
and you love me?

In Contradiction, I am Home

One.

One time
Once
A moment

Stop.

Believer
Bewildered
Delusional

Now.

Yes
No
I don't know.

Pleading.

All at once
I am.

All the same
I am.

All together
I am.

In contradiction
I am home.

I Am Love

Quiet and unassuming
vast and devilishly keen.
Victorious through peace,
dedicated to the cause, the cause,
the cause.

The divine will increase
carefully cultivate
circular enhancements of
thriving possibilities.

Ride with me!

Blazes across my sky.

I am Love! I am Love!

Ride with me.

I Know Why Hemingway Wrote

It's waking up
cracking open guilty eyes
close them! Ouch…

For shame
crawling up my naked back
pelting head and beating mistakes
damn bottles, scattered about.

I know why Hemingway wrote in the morning.

Lilting words
rocking from my pen

Get me high, imagination

Heavy storytelling
this drug tingles
makes me stronger

(What an adrenaline junky)

That's a rush!
This day got better

So, yeah.

I know why Hemingway wrote in the morning.

I Will Break You

Old one!

Long you've walked here.

And as your bones become brittle

And your muscles soften,
as your tongue ties your experience
and your weary eyes droop

I
      Will
            Break you.

For long you've walked here.

I will shred the shoes off your feet

I will turn your pockets out
so you have not even lint
to roll between your fingers.

And still, you will trudge on.

For long you've walked here.

INGRID TURNER

I will rot the teeth out of your head

I will burn your eyes to blind you.

I will stuff thistles in your ears.

You
     Will
          Bleed.

And still, you'll carry on.

For long you've walked here.

I will kill your friends

I will tell lies to your children.

I will plant indifference
in your lover's heart.

And still, you will carry on.

For long you've walked here.

And then I will break your ankles
so you fall to your knees.

And then I will break your hips
so you fall to the ground.

WORDS.LOVE

And when you summon your final strength

To roll on your back to gasp your last breath

(for long you've walked here)

I will bring the stars down to you!

I will massage light into your skin

I will bathe you in diamonds.

I will plant the moon in your heart

I will gift you The North Star.

Your teeth will shine as alabaster shells

Your hair will drop with thick midnight scent

And your clothes will be made from sea spun yarn.

I will pull all the heavens down for you!

And I will

Laboriously

Birth you anew.

But first:

I
    Will
        Break you.

I'll Meet You in Poetry

Somewhere

Over stars and under waves
blazing across that deep black sky

I'll meet you in poetry.

I'm blowing words while I wait;
whistling them out in vibrant

Pinks and blues
splat! on sticky white.

You were grinning last I looked:

A canyon wide and a valley deep.

But now, over my shoulder
you've gone opaque and turned away.

I don't think you're smiling any
more.

Meet me in poetry!
Here's a spot for you.

Take a brush and whittle this prose.

Why don't you stay?
You love it here.

It's Better from a Distance

I have a friend who has it all:
an attentive husband
diamonds on her hands
and pearls around her neck.

I saw them out for dinner one night
he pulled out her chair
and kissed her cheek

And I pretended not to look
pretended not to care.

I told her the next day
I saw you out with him

You look so happy.

I'd die to be you, lady.

She said
it's better from a distance.

That cheek kissing,
and chair pulling,
there's a price, dear.

I have to call ahead
and not be out too late.
I can't have too many friends
or he'll feel bad.

WORDS.LOVE

But I can't give it up
she said

What if no one else loves me?

I'd rather be you
she said
free to roam
free to be.

I smiled at her and I said

It's better from a distance.

I have more room in my bed
but I get cold at night.

I don't have to answer to,
but I don't have a connection either

To share and swear
and sweat and bleed.

I'd give it up
I said, I guess
if it was right.

One day
on a job
I met a woman

With willowy legs
pouty lips,
a star-dazzled smile.

She whisks on through with
a body that curves
and shudders.

She walks on glitter
in stilettos

All the pretty boys
and the ugly ones, too
they look at her
and heave a sigh.

Guess I do, too.

In her presence
(when I found my voice)
I said
you're so lovely

I'd die to be
as lovely as you.

And she curled her glossy lips
and smiled at me.

She said
it's better from a distance.

I don't want this wretched body.
I'm losing my soul

but I can't give it up
she said

Or they won't love me.

WORDS.LOVE

(even when she cried
she was lovely)

I'd rather be you,
she said
and live free
to be me.

And I almost,
I very nearly replied

It's better from a distance.

But, instead

I closed my mouth
put my hand on her back
and I cried too.

It's Not That

It's not that you hold my hand while we walk.
It's that you want to.

It's not the texture of your lips brushing on my back,

It's the dedication behind every kiss.

It's not your mouth on mine,
fervent, hot, needing.

It's your hands cupping my cheeks
reverberating, 'I want this…'

It's not the reassurances that you love me,
through words, through actions.

It's the confusion on your face
when I worry that I'm 'too much'.

It's not the meals you prepare,
under heat and glaze,

But the way you look up at me
while you're stirring.

It's not the sex,
titillating in its newness.

It's the palpitations of this soul
love

pushing into me.

It's not the moments we spend together,

But the necessity of each moment.

It's not the things you do

Or the whispers in the dark

Or the playing

Or the fighting

Or the crazy vows we're already making.

It's that you want this too,
just as bad as I do.

Joey

On a normal day
you seem very heavy.
You can get in the way
and you can be so needy.

I pick you up
I feel the weight
and think, damn this is hard.
Just wait, Joey, wait!

Then we laughed today
loud, belly rolling giggles
I scooped you up in all your wriggles
laughing, and swinging this way

And you seem very light, indeed.

Johanna

Just a little
over sensitive, perhaps, but
have such a heart
and you seem in life
nervous, a little,
needy, a little, yet
amorous and extreme.

Sympathetic, Johanna,
big brown eyes
deep thought and empathy
radiates from those eyes.

Dreamer, Johanna,
white knight is around the corner
isn't he? Isn't he?
He'll sweep you away
take you places on Earth
that don't exist in Heaven.
Of course true love exists.

Righteous, Johanna,
keep the light in sight,
don't hurt each other
keep the kindness intact
man was born to love.
...wasn't he?

Sensitive, Johanna,
don't understand why
he treated me like that.
he does love me, it's just...
he just...
there must be a reason.

Strength, Johanna.
You overcame it
you said 'no more!'
you will not follow that bloody line.
No child of yours
will feel like you.

Johanna, Johanna,
beautiful Johanna,
fight on Johanna,
and fight on with no loss
of the sympathetic,
the dreamer, the righteous
the sensitive girl
that molded our beautiful Johanna.

Just Between You and Me

Do you remember?
Remember the day?
That time we played
just you and me?

I remember
long time ago now:
we touched fingertip-to-fingertip.
It was *electric*, friend!

All the possibilities of creation
crackled between our fingers
what a reflection!
That flash in your eyes.

Who turned away first?
Was it you? Was it me?
Who left those possibilities
sputtering in the dirt?

Laughing in the Sky

If I could still hear you
I bet I'd hear

Laughing, laughing
way up in the sky.

I bet it echoes
through cosmos and ages

I bet it rolls and rumbles
bellying over the winds

And crashing through tides.
I can almost hear

If I listen very hard

Laughing
Laughing

Way up high.

WORDS.LOVE

Love Robs Me of Words

I love you.

I *love* you.

I love you!

I am a proud wordsmith.

But standing in front of you I dig

and I dig for the words
and they just grind in my throat.

That's how I win them all over, you know.
It's with my words.

Lyricism is the honey
I catch all the flies with.

But words are not enough for you.

I am stuck and stammering
in love

And that seems to be
where my words go to die.

And I am afraid of this!

Words have never failed me

But they just won't do for you.

Now I sit
with this soup of

Fears and tears and love.

And...

That's it, isn't it?

Love.

Full stop.

Me Loving Me

...me
...loving
...me

Full stop.

If I could show you an easy life

It would be

Solid
...in your skin.

INGRID TURNER

Monster Attacks a City

I wasn't asleep when it came
though I may as well have been.

It didn't arrive suddenly:
no stomping buildings, gnashing
teeth.

The Monster seeped in
while I was wide awake.

No shattered skyscrapers:
no buckled concrete.

It was a quiet kind of sinister:
skittering along the shadows.

No smoky explosions:
no flaming breath, deafening roars.

This Monster brushed its teeth,
stretched its neck, straightened it's
tie.

I felt no trembling Earth.
I heard no lusty roar.

While I lumbered through my morning
and sucked on bitter beans

The Monster went quietly to work
and, with a smile, ruined my day.

My Beautiful Things

To my crystals and candles
my pendulum and cards

My flowers and my Buddha
my little notes and prayers

To my pictures and memories
my softly lit backdrop

To my sweet incense
and pungent sage

How lovingly we have interacted

Through light fingers and deep breaths

What comfort you've brought me
through the gates of doubt

What relief I've found
in your immovability

To my beautiful things
that have held my faith

When I could not hold my own.

One-Way Ticket

'It's a one-way ticket to paradise',
he said.
'You won't want to come back,' he
assured.
He cocked his head, and toothed a
grin
nudging me toward the train.

I got to paradise, alright.
And paradise is dry.
And thirsty. And a little bitter.

The train dropped me off in Mojave
someone's adobe idea
of bone peace, I guess.

I wish I could get back to greener
pastures
with moisture for my cracked lips
and barrels of rain for my raspy
throat.

Promised me someone else's dream
and *they* never wanted to leave.
'It'll be yours too,' he said,
With a Grandfatherly wink.

So, he offered me a one-way ticket
(which I took)
Because I believed.

Our Fight

A lump in my throat

Nausea.

It's still cool this early.
A slammed door drops like thunder.

Half of me wants to scream.
The other half: stunned into silence.

It's been one of those fights
where I don't know if I'll ever see
you again.

Piano

There's hesitation in your fingers.

Halting, careful. Treading thin.

Elton John is at one shoulder
I'm at the other.

(It's ok.
You can play).

Cracking, for a moment
your voice rises.

Just a little
and fingers maybe glide

Sing with Elton:

*'You see I've forgotten
if they're green or blue'*

(definitely blue).

And then you shift
to a New York State of mind

With Billy Joel at your back.
Chaos in harmony.

WORDS.LOVE

Now you've cocked a grin,
a sideways glance at me:

(Hello, my love).

Feeling it now,
fingers dashing, body rocking.

That's when you and Randy
take me to Louisiana.

'They're trying to wash us away.'

(To Cape Arago)?

Ah!

Remember?
It was kind of like this.

We stepped out of time,
and danced along the edge of forever.

Prayer

In joy
I sing your name

In agony
I scream at you

In grief
I beg for you

But always, always
I call for you

Quit

I would love
to be
held and adored
squeezed and reassured
lilted to perfection
given a new perception
by you.

But,
failing all that
I'd really like
to smoke a cigarette.

Rebel

I am a rebel!

But you'd never know it.

You couldn't pick me out of a crowd
'that one is different!'

Not in any tangible way.

I don't wear clothes
that brand me 'rebel'.

You don't see me holding signs
or pumping my fists.

I probably won't be yelling at you

(unless I'm singing your praises).

I'm not going to chain myself to a tree
but I might be hugging it.

No:

My rebellion runs deeper.

WORDS.LOVE

It's not defined by tribal doctrine
no matter how fringe.

My rebellion is quiet.

It's stealthy, subtle

Changing your life
without you even knowing it.

My rebellion is the rebellion of
Love!

The flashiest it gets
is my flashing smile

And the rest of my rabble rousing
is dancing in my heart.

Rings

You didn't put a ring on it
because your ring was around my heart
and my ring was around your heart.

And baby,
when we came together in that embrace
we clasped so tight
those rings, they fused together
and our hearts,
they started to beat together

Boom
      Boom
            Boom

And when you got sick
I got sick too.

You lay in that hospital bed
and I said
this hurts me, baby,
my heart's in pain.
      You may not die!

And you hoarsed:

      'Babe, you can't tell me what
to do any more.

            But I love you.'

WORDS.LOVE

And then you died.
After all I demanded,
after all I begged
    'Baby!
        This hurts!'

Silence.

But our hearts were still fused
together

See,

and while yours had stopped,

mine
    mine
        mine was still beating.

Our hearts are still held together
with rusty rings
and now I'm pumping that sick
all through my body
and I'm dying

    I'm dying
        without the satisfaction

of death.

Because baby,

    my heart's fused with a dead
man's.

Savior

Oh, we do forget

Even our saviors
 are confused.

Siren Song

I don't care what song
that siren sings.

There's no lure attached to me.

So sing on raucous minx!

I love the way this watery ballad
makes me sway.

Stasis No More

I'll be still in dreams
no more.

I'll resist the unbelievable
no more.

Today I crouch one time
to fly.

Today's last breath comes
to fly.

Now I live.
Now I live.

Stasis no more.

Lady!

You drive a hard bargain against
defeat.

Life twists us all up
in her gnarled branches

And you, dear;

You spin right out
with a triumphal curtsy.

Lady,

You are Cheshire Cat in the face of
overwhelm.

Chaos catches us all
in her slippery whirlpool.

But you, dear:

Use just a finger
to turn the tide.

Lady, lady:

You are draped in silver and jewels,
I swear!

And I could always tell you
how much I admire

Your grace
Your talent
Your fierce
Your pride.

But I'd rather just sit with you, I think

And wrap myself with a corner of your silver.

Swallows Her Tears

Baby girl
Chubby cheeks
Playing in mud
Delighted squeals

'Stop!'
Mother tells
Baby starts
Fearful cries.

'No, no, no!'
Picks her up
Drops in tub

'We don't play

in the mud'
'Shhh, stop crying!'

Baby girl swallows her tears.

Little girl
Runs at school
Falls on asphalt
Blood on tights.

'Little girl. What is this?'
'You've ruined your clothes'
'Stop crying.'

Stop bleeding.

Little girl swallows her tears.

Young lady
Standing stiff
Old man
Smells like barley

'Stand still!'
'Don't fidget!'
'Wrong tone!'
Be straight. Be perfect.

Young lady swallows her tears.

Young woman
On a stage
Finds the voice
She swallowed whole.

Tears are flowing
Song is ringing

The hall coos
'Yes child.'
'It's safe here.'
'Let it go, let it go.'

WORDS.LOVE

Thunderous applause
a few shaking heads.

Reviews said
'She shouldn't have cried.'
'There's potential, tone it down.'
'She lost control.'

She sang
When she couldn't scream.

Young woman swallows her tears.

'No more songs!'
She vows
Eyes dry.

And the grieving halls
They ache
Oh, they ache.

Sweet Surrender

Sweet Surrender;

Why do you avoid me?

I peer around buildings
just to glimpse you flitting around
the next

I hear only echoes of your laughter
but my belly is empty of joy.

I follow this worn path to you
but kneel weeping over dried
footprints.

Sweet surrender:
I cannot but chase after you!

Longing for your arms to steady me

To steady me
To steady me

But long instead I journey on
and loud instead I wail on

WORDS.LOVE

Calling, calling your name

Surrender! Surrender!

But you do not speak.
You do not listen.

Until exhausted, I collapse along the way

And only in the black depths of my sleep

When I cannot see you
When I cannot hear you
When I cannot need you

Do you finally, finally caress me.

That Scent

Why do I smell you?

It's been months since I've seen you.
Longer since I touched you.

It's your cologne, clinging
to my clothes, wafting through the
air.

Subtly rich, and sweet; lingering,
like pipe tobacco.

Why do I smell you?

How long has it been since I kissed
you?
I don't even miss you, really.

Except, why do I smell you?

There's a hint of sweat, all mixed
in.
Acrid. Nostalgic.

Reminds me of sex with you.

That scent! It's hugging my sleeves
sitting in the car next to me.

Brushing my hair.

Why do I smell you?
I don't even fucking like you.

The Flowers Are Pink

The flowers you bought me are pink.

Pastel.
Friendly.

Of course, I want to exclaim delight

But the fact of the matter is
the flowers you bought me are pink.

Pastel.
Friendly.

What drew you to these in the store?

Absent-minded thoughtfulness?

Pink says:

Chatty.
Surface.

Let's keep it light.

Our whole life is pink.

Don't you see me craving red?

Deep.
Carnal.

Can't you see through my pretty smile
to my husky needs?

Do you not see my jaw clenching?

Do you not see my hands
scraping along my needy thighs?

Why are you set on pink?

Pastel.
Friendly.

When I'm dripping with red over here.

The Man and The Genie

The genie said to the man:

'I'll grant you one wish!
What will it be?

I've made kings and Gods
and I alone
made the most beautiful woman
the world has known.

I've ended hunger and plague;
I've won holy wars
and brought back the dead.

So, what will it be, simple man?

What wish lies in the dark?
What is held so deeply within?

What is hidden from all you know?
That I alone can bring to light
and make more real than real?'

The man responded:

'I have no dark wish, Genie,
only darkness.

If you can banish my longing,
nothing else I'll ever need.

Genie, oh genie,
what I crave is this:

Let me know God!

Let me bathe in His glory,
let me know His love.

Let me see Him wherever I go,
let me be the one
to bestow His grace.

Let me awaken, Genie,
into spiritual ecstasy.

Let me be enlightened.

Let me

      Finally

          Be

with God eternally.

This, oh Genie, is my greatest wish.'

Stillness within the quiet.

Genie looked at Man
and Man, looked at Genie.

Waiting.
Contemplating.

'Your wish',
Genie finally said

'Is my command.'

A bang, a blast!

WORDS.LOVE

Genie was gone
and Man stood alone.

And nothing had changed.

Time in Love

They say that time flies

When you're having fun.

But my experience with you, darling,
is the other way around.

With you, time slows and becomes
graceful.

The moments connect with gentle
touches

The hours sigh deeply with pleasure

The days pirouette with the sudden
illusion of speed

Only to slow to near stillness

And a perfect hold.

Time flies perhaps with fun

But with you,

WORDS.LOVE

My darling,

In love,

Time is held breath
in almost unbearable pleasure.

Today, I Walk with the Lord

I walk with the Lord today.

Yesterday I was a wild witch
running beside pagan wolves.

Today I burned the bitch at the
stake.

Tomorrow looks good for mourning
Jesus is crucified tonight.

I'm not sure what I am next.

Perhaps you'll find me draped in the
ocean.
or maybe I'll flit along each star.

Tip-toe one, tip-toe two…

I may proudly soar with the eagle
or skulk and shiver with the rat.

I can spread all this out by days
or hours, or minutes.

Mostly you'll see me kneeling

In prayer?
In jest?

In desperate, desperate

(dear God)
Connection.

Tribute to a Troubled Father

What should have been
baby blues and pumpkin spices

For you dad

Was black and blue
and terrorizes.

All those years
you clenched it so tight.

Blowing and caving
losing and winning the fight.

I know dad.

I've got the hang of it now.
I'm choosing baby blues

And your grandson,
He'll taste pumpkin spice, too.

And your granddaughters;
they own their choice.

So, thank you, dad,
for the fights you won.

And thank you dad,
for the fights you lost.

I'm winning the war now.
For you. For us.

Two Become One

Two become one.

Instinct and Spirit

Fight and fawn

Fierce and frail

Two become one

With graceful age.

Look at this!

Outrageous beauty
in one man.

Untitled

On dizzying heights
or in gasping lows

It is only ever the depth of experience.

Sink into madness
rise in exalted form.

Catch the sky with your breath.

What you seek lurks deep
quivering in anticipation of you.

When the Dawn Breaks

Don't be afraid

It's only the darkness before the dawn.

And when the dawn breaks
and when the dawn breaks

It will be glorious. Dazzling.
Brazen and beautiful

Unbearable. Even
in its brilliance.

Do not despair
your eyes will adjust.

Trudge on! Trudge on!

Just a little more.

The daylight breaks
just over the hill.

It's coming! It's coming!

The dawn is here.

Wretched

The bough of agony
swings mighty

Brings me thundering to my knees.

And it is in the billowing
of my pain

Whistling
along my howls

Gushing
from my eyes

Retching
in my stomach

I open now

To exquisite
Infinite.

There she rests
serenely

Just a sleeping babe
under my bosom.

A place to love

Now

My heart finally cleansed
of wretched shame.

You Can't Bottle Magic

You can't bottle magic.

But every night
when the wizard yawns

We try again.

WORDS.LOVE

INGRID TURNER

WORDS.LOVE

'Locked in Love'

'Locked in Love' by Psychic Medium Ingrid Turner is a compilation of channeled messages from divine spirit, offering guidance, transformation, and spiritual connection. Available now on Amazon: bit.ly/lockedinlove

www.ingramcontent.com/pod-product-compliance
Lightning Source LLC
Chambersburg PA
CBHW060846050426
42453CB00008B/846